USING THIS BOOK

Now We're Talking! is primarily a resource for parents, to help cultivate stronger relationships with preschoolers, grade-schoolers, and teenagers.

Great questions, however, are an invaluable aid to anyone who spends time with children, such as:

- **Grandparents** who want to venture into the worlds of their grandchildren;
- **Teachers** who want to launch meaningful discussions with their students;
- **Youth ministers** and workers who want to engage the hearts and minds of the young people they serve;
- **Counselors** who want to unlock the significant issues in the lives of troubled children; and
- **Baby-sitters** who are motivated to do more than merely "watch the kids."

Questions That
Bring You Closer
to Your Kids

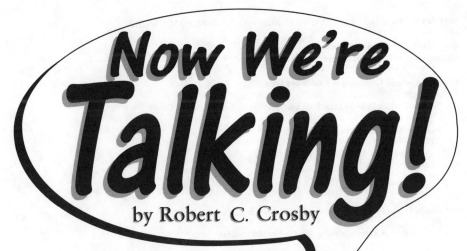

Now We're Talking!

by Robert C. Crosby

Questions That Bring You Closer to Your Kids

Colorado Springs, Colorado

NOW WE'RE TALKING! QUESTIONS THAT BRING YOU CLOSER TO YOUR KIDS

Copyright © 1996 by Robert C. Crosby
All rights reserved. International copyright secured.

Library of Congress Cataloging-in-Publication Data
Crosby, Robert C.
    Now we're talking : questions that bring you closer to your kids / Robert C. Crosby.
        p. cm.
    Includes bibliographical references.
    ISBN 1-56179-472-4
    1. Parent and child—Miscellanea. I. Title.
HQ755.85.C76   1996
306.874—dc20

96-21531
CIP

Published by Focus on the Family Publishing, Colorado Springs, Colorado 80995.

Distributed in the U.S.A. and Canada by Word Books, Dallas, Texas.

Unless otherwise indicated, Scripture taken from the HOLY BIBLE, NEW INTERNATIONAL VERSION ®, (NIV) ®. Copyright © 1973, 1978, 1984 by International Bible Society. Used by permission of Zondervan Publishing House. All rights reserved.

Focus on the Family books are available at special quantity discounts when purchased in bulk by corporations, organizations, churches, or groups. Special imprints, messages, and excerpts can be produced to meet your needs. For more information, contact: Sales Dept., Focus on the Family Publishing, 8605 Explorer Dr., Colorado Springs, CO 80920; or phone (719) 531-3400.

Editor: Colorado Wordmaster
Cover Designer: Candi L. Park

Printed in the United States of America

96 97 98 99 00 01 02 03/10 9 8 7 6 5 4 3 2 1

To Pamela,
my soul mate and
partner in parenting.

How I thank God
for the question I asked
and the answer you gave.

CONTENTS

Introduction

ASKING GREAT QUESTIONS

Art Linkletter captured the hearts of millions 35 years ago when he tried something on television that no one else was doing—asking children questions. He carved out a niche for himself and fascinated his audience by giving children the microphone while the adults sat back and listened.

Linkletter summed up his motivation in his book *Kids Say the Darnedest Things:* "There's a vast gulf between the world of children and our own. And every time we bridge that gulf—even if it's only for a moment—we recapture some of the freshness and spontaneity that make life worth living."[1]

Questions are one of the most effective yet perhaps most underused tools in a parent's toolbox today. Just five minutes of expressing interest in your child will do more to build your relationship with him/her than five months of trying to get him/her interested in you.

If you're like me, however, you easily get stuck in the gear of telling your kids what to do, telling them how to do it, and telling them when to do it, instead of taking time to ask meaningful questions. To most of us, parenting means telling, not asking.

Without a doubt, parenting does involve imparting. You cannot visit the Bible's paramount parenting passages of Deuteronomy 6 or Ephesians 6 without catching the action verbs of child-rearing: "impress," "love," "train," "encourage," and "comfort." However, parenting also includes drawing out from within the heart of your child. A great question draws upon openness, honesty, cooperation, and friendship. King Solomon put it this way: "The purposes of a man's heart are deep waters, but a man of understanding *draws* them out" (Prov. 20:5, emphasis added).

Ambassadors use questions to build bridges between countries that are oceans apart. Teachers use questions to build bridges to their students. Spouses use questions to build intimacy with one another. Managers use question to cultivate teamwork and productivity among employees. Wise parents use questions to bridge the generation divide with their children, whether en route to nursery school or on the way home from a high school soccer game.

As clearly as an invitation beckons a friend to attend a birthday party, bridal shower, or backyard barbecue, questions invite people in. They evoke a response. Questions engage the individual. Effectively formed and sensitively placed, they construct an atmosphere of interest that draws upon the hidden resources and needs of the soul.

Heading home from a full day of pastoral duties that

climaxed with our weekly youth group meeting at an inner-city church, I was rubbing my eyes and trying to stay awake enough to keep the Plymouth Horizon between the lines.

Suddenly, a little voice pierced the silence. My four-year-old, Kristin, said, "So . . . Daddy . . . what did you do today?"

I really didn't feel like talking. Still, my conscience reminded me that this little girl and I hadn't spoken much at all since the day before. On top of that, she was giving this bridge-building effort her best shot. How could I resist?

"Well, sweetie . . . Dad studied and met with some people and made some phone calls and spoke at the youth meeting tonight."

Then a follow-up question came to mind that I had never asked my daughter before. I decided to give it a try.

"Kristi, what does Daddy do?" She probably thought I did nothing but stand in front of groups of people and run my mouth all day. I waited.

Kristi scrunched up her brow a bit and then said, "Hmm . . . you sing . . . and you teach . . . kids . . . how to love Jesus!"

Instantly, my brain went into high gear. I wanted to shout, *Bulls-eye! Kristin Anne Crosby, you hit the nail right on the head!* I was suddenly energized with this four-year-old's insight.

So much of our adult lives we struggle to find the simple focus of what we want to do or, more important, what we feel called to do. Not the many "good" things, but the one great thing. Here it was, in one seven-word reply to a question: *You teach kids how to love Jesus!*

I couldn't help rewarding her with a stop at McDonald's.

That was the moment I began to discover the incredible tool of simply asking great questions. That was the start of an adventure I am still on today.

To me, having children and not asking them questions is like having an easel and never getting out the paints. The best a child has to offer is often bottled up deep within.

Parenting at its best is much more than getting children through school, teaching them responsibility, and raising them to be law-abiding citizens. Parenting is about opening a soul, freeing a spirit, unleashing a life brimming with potential to discover all God has intentioned.

The first section of this book, "The Quest," is full of ideas, principles, and examples of how great questions can be used to reach a child. The second part, "The Questions," offers all kinds of great questions you can ask your preschooler, grade-schooler, and teenager to enrich their lives—and find your own soul replenished.

Before we go any further, I would like to acknowledge the assistance I received in this venture of faith.

Deep appreciation goes to Dean Merrill, Al Janssen, and everyone at Focus on the Family for giving a new kid on the block a shot at a dream. Hats off to Brad Lewis for challenging me to write and rewrite, to think and rethink. Lots of love to my life partner, Pam, for encouraging me even when the inkwell was dry. High fives to all the teenagers who were a part of Vineyard Youth Ministries in Rochester, New York, in the '80s . . . you guys were always up for my questions. Most of all, deep affection for four little Crosbys—Kristin, Kara, Robbi, and Kandace. I have only begun to ask!

Notes

1. As quoted in Dandi Daley Mackall, *Kids Are Still Saying the Darnedest Things* (Rocklin, Calif.: Prime Publishing, 1944), p. xii.

Part One

The Quest

*I praise you, Father, Lord of heaven and earth,
because you have hidden these things from
the wise and learned, and revealed them to
little children.*

Jesus
(Matt. 11:25)

Chapter One

TWELVE BENEFITS
OF ASKING QUESTIONS

The spoken question is . . .
the most popular piece of language
for adults, and by far
the favorite with kids.

Gerald Goodman[1]

Salesmen ask questions because they want to make a sale. Teachers ask questions because they want to open minds. Police detectives ask questions because they want to solve crimes.

Here are at least a dozen reasons why a parent should always have a ready supply of strategic questions to ask children:

1. Questions show your genuine interest in the child. Merely saying, "I love you" or "I really care about you" is not enough. When parents care enough to frame a well-suited question and patiently tap what may interest or concern the child, they open more than a conversation. They may open a soul.

2. Questions assure your child that you really care about what he/she thinks and feels. We tend to trust people who are tuned in to our needs enough to be concerned about them . . . and who respect us enough to hold those sacred trusts in confidence. Parents have an unparalleled opportunity to do both.

Too often, we are quick to deny something that is very real to our children. For example, when my young son realizes it is bedtime, he may start to cry and say, "I don't want to go to bed. I'm scared."

What is my typical response as a dad? "No, you're not. You're not scared! You're a big boy."

In that moment, instead of acknowledging his felt emotion and helping him deal with it, I whip out the "remote control" and, in essence, say, *Turn that feeling off right now. That is not acceptable. I don't have time to deal with it. Be brave!*

I could never get away with treating an adult that way. Why do I think I can do so with a fragile child?

3. Questions model good social skills for the child.

Every child, teenager, and adult for that matter, is ill-prepared to face life if he/she doesn't know how to ask good questions. Parents who ask their children great questions strengthen the relational skills of their kids, saving them needless days, if not months and years, of uncertainty, loneliness, and insecurity in social settings.

I had the chance to watch my five-year-old daughter on one of her first days at kindergarten. While the other children were playing together, she kept to herself.

After school, I asked Kristin, "How was your class today? Did you enjoy it?"

"No one would be friends with me, Dad."

"Really?"

"Uh-uh. They all played together and wouldn't let me in."

It was obvious she was perplexed and discouraged. So I said, "Kristi, what did you do to try and make friends?"

"I waited for them to come play with me, and no one ever did."

"Well, did you ask them anything?"

"No, but they don't like me. None of them do. I don't want to go tomorrow."

I didn't try to refute her opinion. I simply said, "Well, sweetheart, I want you to try something tomorrow. I think that if you will ask them some questions, you might be able to make friends with one or two of the other kids. Everybody likes to be asked questions about themselves. That's the best way I know to make friends."

"What questions, Dad?"

Together we came up with five questions she could take to school the next day:

"What is your name?"

"What is your favorite game to play? . . . cartoon to watch? . . . food to eat?"

"How many brothers and sisters do you have? What are their names?"

"Do you have any pets at home? What kind? What are their names?"

"What would you like to play?"

I took a leap of faith and assured Kristin that if she would use these questions and others that came to mind, she would begin to make friends.

The next afternoon, my daughter came out of school with a big smile plastered across her face. "Dad, it worked!"

As Dale Carnegie put it: "To be interesting, you must be interested."

4. Questions let you find out just how much of your parental training is taking root. We spend so much time pouring into our children's lives that it makes sense to see if they're actually embracing any of it.

One of the most fun ways is to play the "What Would You Do If?" game:

"What if you were taking a test, and the teacher walked out of the room? Let's say that you were sitting next to the smartest kid in the class and you could easily see his answers. What would you do?"

Your child's response to such a question may tell you a lot about where he/she is in moral development.

5. Questions bring focus to your time with your child, rather than just wasting the hours. Seize the spontaneous moments here and there . . . the ride to school in the morning, the last-minute trip to the grocery store, tucking them into bed at night, standing in line at a checkout stand, halftime at a football game. These can be just as fruitful as the organized "quality times" you plan.

6. Questions help you discern your child's true emotional and spiritual needs. Without asking questions, no parent should expect to truly know his/her child's greatest needs *today*, as opposed to yesterday or a month ago.

7. Questions often create a sense of need within your child for principles and insights that you are

uniquely equipped to teach. Great questions can evoke a topic that's truly important.

We waste our time putting a plate of prime rib in front of a child who has just finished a plate of lasagna. In like manner, sometimes the best way to teach a child is to create or discover a hunger within him/her for wisdom.

Wise parents and teachers for centuries have recognized the power of asking great questions:

> One of the greatest teachers of all time was Socrates, who lived in Athens from 470 to 399 B.C. His list of pupils and their students-in-turn includes Plato, who taught Aristotle, who taught Alexander the Great. Socrates' reputation in the fifth century B.C. as the wisest man in the world was based upon his own claim that among all men he was the most aware of his own ignorance,

thereby making him the wisest! His method of teaching others depended on asking them questions, hoping by this means to open his students' minds by driving them to a deeper consideration of the issues. . . . But always the point of asking a question was to show how much more of a subject remains to be learned.[2]

8. Questions inspire your child to think through and establish his/her own values and standards for living. Jesus used questions powerfully to challenge His followers. He interspersed no fewer than 14 questions in the Sermon on the Mount:

> If the salt loses its saltiness, how can it be made salty again?
> If you love those who love you, what reward will you get? Are not even the tax

collectors doing that? And if you greet only your brothers, what are you doing more than others? Do not even pagans do that?

Is not life more important than food, and the body more important than clothes? Look at the birds of the air; they do not sow or reap or store away in barns, and yet your heavenly Father feeds them. Are you not much more valuable than they? Who of you by worrying can add a single hour to his life?

And why do you worry about clothes? . . . If that is how God clothes the grass of the field, . . . will he not much more clothe you, O you of little faith?

Why do you look at the speck of sawdust in your brother's eye and pay no attention to the plank in your own eye?

Which of you, if his son asks for bread, will give him a stone? Or if he asks for a fish, will give him a snake?

Do people pick grapes from thornbushes, or figs from thistles? (Matt. 5–7)

9. Questions cultivate intimacy between parent and child. Considerate questions draw a child closer. They slow us down in our much-too-busy lifestyles and build bridges of interest that often turn to feelings of bondedness.

10. Questions clarify what the child actually had in mind. Questions keep us from jumping to false conclusions . . . questions such as:

"How did you feel when that happened?"

"What would you have done differently if you could do this over?"

"What do you think caused this to happen?"

11. Questions bring your child's dreams and desires close enough to the surface for you to affirm and encourage them. Whom does your daughter most admire? What heroes does your son often think about? What accomplishments do they dream of? What are their highest hopes and greatest aspirations? Parents may never know until they ask.

12. Questions are "education" in the truest sense of the word. "Education" comes from the Latin word *educare,* which means "to draw forth." Most of us do too much stuffing things in and not enough drawing things forth. Instead of saying, "Well, that's what you get!" we need to say, "Oh, that's interesting. What happened? Let's talk about that. How do you feel about it?" Or, "What did you learn from it?"

God only knows the potential, the ideas, the dreams, and the hopes wrapped up in the soul of a child. Parents get to nudge open those souls and watch them grow, emerging as individuals made in God's image. Questions are the essential tool in this process.

Notes

1. Gerald Goodman, *The Talk Book* (New York: Ballantine, 1988), p. 131.

2. D. Bruce Lockerbie, *Asking Questions* (Milford, Mich.: Mott Media, 1980), p. 23.

Chapter Two

SHARPENING THE TOOL

*The main reason questions are so effective is
that most people love to answer them. . . .
How else can you explain the continued
popularity of question-and-answer
quiz shows on radio and television?*

Dorothy Leeds[1]

If you've ever asked someone, "So, how was your day?" and gotten a mumbled "Okay" in reply, you know that some questions work better than others.

What is the difference between a great question and a dead-end question? Often the substance is solid, but the edges are not nearly sharp enough.

CLOSED AND OPEN QUESTIONS

Closed questions are those that can be handled briefly: "Yes," "No," "Good," "Bad," or "Okay." They fail to draw on the person's imagination or genuine feelings.

Open, or *sharpened*, questions are those that elicit a full response. Here are some examples:

CLOSED	OPEN
"How are you doing?"	"If you had to describe how you're feeling as a weather report, would you say you're feeling sunny, cloudy, partly

sunny, partly cloudy, or
what? What do you think is
making you feel that way?"

"Are you building   "Which of your friends at
good friendships   school are you the most like?
at school?"   In what way? Which are you
                           the most unlike? How so?"

On America's frontier during the nineteenth century, Quaker families collectively developed four great questions that were regularly used in small groups to get acquainted with newly arriving settlers. It is obvious that these questions were not just off-the-cuff but were carefully, if not prayerfully, thought through. They were so effective that some small groups today still use them:

1. "When you were 10 years old, how was your house heated?"

2. "What was the warmest room in your house?"

3. "Who were you closest to?"

4. "When did God become more than just a name to you?"

There is a flow to this set of questions that creates openness. They move from general to personal, from above the "waterline" to below, without threatening anyone.

HOW TO SHARPEN A QUESTION

Here are a few key principles to keep in mind as you frame your own questions:

1. Ask questions that cannot be answered with a mere "yes" or "no." Don't just ask for an opinion; ask for a reason for the opinion.

2. Be precise. I can't count how many times I have been asked, "What do you think is God's will for

your life?" I've always found that question too broad
for me to tackle. But I will never forget the time
someone asked me the same question in a different
way: "If you could do anything you wanted to do for
the kingdom of God, and be guaranteed it would succeed, what would you do?"

Wow! Now that is one excitingly specific question. It
digs deep and draws out the dreams within me.

3. Go "below the waterline." In other words, get
underneath the trivial and open the soul.

Our kids are naturally primed to talk about
movies, music, sports, and hobbies. However, sometimes they need most to talk about their fears, their
friendships, their dreams, their failures, their hopes,
their anger, their hurt. The wise parent learns to
carefully navigate a conversation from the trivial to
the important, from matters of the mind to matters
of the heart.

Here is a set of steps that begins with lighter fare and moves progressively deeper.

Favorites — From sports teams to breakfast cereal to music to movies, almost everyone enjoys talking about his/her favorites.

Fun — Discover something that your child genuinely enjoys, and ask about it. Seek out his/her bank of knowledge, experiences, and dreams in this area.

Friends — Sorting out relationships, how they work and how they don't, is something every child needs help doing.

Feelings — Checking the temperature of your child's soul and the reasons for it is a great way to show love and concern.

Failures — Parents who can patiently wait through the impulse reactions of their children when they struggle and stumble in life are then positioned to help their children just talk about it. This is a great service.

Fears — The things that usually hurt and haunt children and teens the most are the things they never talk about to anyone. Few parents get to this juncture with their kids.

The Future — A teen's senior year in high school is not the first time he/she needs to approach this topic. From the earliest years, children need to be asked about their dreams, hopes, and aspirations. When we ask about these things, we encourage them to soar.

Faith — Many children are exposed to spiritual instruction from Sunday school teachers, youth workers, and pastors. How many parents, however, provide a regular diet of questions designed to nurture and challenge their children toward spiritual growth?

4. Inquire, don't interrogate. Your child's spirit will quickly close if he/she perceives you as a prosecutor. Such questions seek to lead the questionee to the questioner's desired end.

Before asking a question, stop and ask yourself: *What attitude or spirit is motivating my question? Am I asking in order to discover or to deride? Does my question sound accusatory or merely inquisitive? Would I want to be asked this question by one of my leaders?*

Simply plowing through a litany of questions will make a child, especially an older one, feel more like an interviewee than a son or daughter. Questions are a seasoning that should fill every great conversation. They should be mixed with advice, encouragement, information, lots of listening, and humor.

5. Use the word "if" a lot. "If you could have any job in the world, which one would you choose?" "If you could visit any place on the planet, where would you go?" "If you could change anything about yourself, what would it be?"

"If" questions are powerful tools for tapping the imagination.

6. Remember, questions beget questions. Once you're "in the front door" of a young person's mind, there is a houseful of furniture and people to discover. Use follow-up questions to discover more about feelings and opinions:

"How long have you felt this way?"

"How does that make you feel?"

"Would you tell me more about this?"

"What do you think about that?"

"How does that affect you?"

"What steps will you take to deal with that?"

"How did you come to this conclusion?"

7. Don't just ask questions; really listen to the answers. It never ceases to amaze me how tuned in kids are to body language and listening disciplines. Kids seem to know whether their answer is being endured, ignored, or enjoyed.

8. Don't force the answer; wait for it. When people forget to mail invitations, no one shows up for the party. When parents fail to ask great questions—or quickly move on to something else—so much of their children's pain and potential remain locked up within their underchallenged minds and souls.

Sharpened questions are the best way I know to tap the treasure. And besides, you will never find out for yourself until you ask . . . will you?

Notes

1. Dorothy Leeds, *Smart Questions* (New York: Berkley Books, 1987), p. 24.

Chapter Three

TIMING IS EVERYTHING

Well-formed, clear questions teach, illuminate ideas, encourage ordered thinking, and reward you with clear answers. Master the art of the question, and you master a source of great power.

Bill Beausay[1]

Moments. Life is full of them. Moments made and moments missed.

Gloria Gaither described the valuable moments in a family's life through a song: "We have this moment to hold in our hands and to touch as it slips through our fingers like sand. Yesterday's gone and tomorrow may never come, but we have this moment today."[2]

Obviously, we cannot force poignant moments with our children. However, we can increase the chances that they will occur. We can be ready to make the most of them when they do. Here are three ways.

WAYS TO ENHANCE LIFE'S MOMENTS

1. Seize the moment. Sometimes moments make themselves. They come unexpectedly and stare us right in the face, literally ripe with opportunity to teach a child.

This is where having a ready arsenal of great questions is crucial. Regardless of the topic or concern you are facing with your child, sharp-edged questions can turn a good moment into a great one. The following are worth committing to memory because they will work in almost any situation:

"What can I do to help?"

"What has to be done?"

"Could you explain a little more?"

"How does that make you feel?"

"Could you tell me what your reason is for asking?"

"What needs to change?"

"What are you trying to accomplish?"

"How can I talk to you so you'll want to talk to me?"

"What do you want?"

"What's happening now?"

"What stops you from getting what you want?"

"What are you going to do about it?"

"What do you need to reach your goal?"

"How will you know if you're moving toward your goal?"[3]

2. Construct the moment. Sometimes moments can be made. One great way to do this is to take this book with you as you tuck kids into bed at night. Let a question be their last impression of the day. Your relationship with them will be warmed and strengthened. And who knows, you may strike pay dirt.

Sometimes one of the best ways for a dad or mom to enhance conversations with his or her children is to *lighten up!* Children's lives can quickly fill with schedules, deadlines, and other people's expectations and requirements. There are moments when what they need most from us is grace.

As adults we can get to be just a bit too dignified, can't we? Learn at times to be silly with kids. Laugh. Put yourself into their world. Remember, a child's world is not five-and-a-half feet tall, it is two-and-a-half feet tall. So be vulnerable. Allow them to laugh with you, even at you. And apologize to your child when you're wrong.

Out of this can come wonderful moments.

3. Cultivate the moment. If you find that, for whatever reason, your conversation with your teen or preteen has suddenly left the trivial level and delved into things more important, don't be quick to leave the subject. Chances are it has come up because deep down, your child really does need to talk.

This is why great follow-up questions come in handy, such as:

"How long have you felt this way?"

"What do you do to deal with these feelings?"

"Do you know other people who share your feelings?"

"Do you think I've ever felt that way?"

"What steps do you plan to take?"

PLACES TO ASK

A parent's world is uniquely provided with golden opportunities to ask their kids questions. Consider a few of the places:

1. Table talk. For generations, the dinner table has been the nucleus of the household, where busy lives slow down for an hour and reconnect under the love and leadership of a mother and father.

Unfortunately, today many homes have moved away from sharing meals as a family to eating in front of a television or, as the kids get older, everyone eating at different times. Consistent meals together at the table are worth fighting for. It's a time when questions can flourish.

One of our favorite games to play at the table as a family begins with my asking a question such as, "Okay, Kara—what were you doing at 11:00 this morning?"

Kara fills us in, and then it is her turn to pick someone else at the table and ask the same question, inserting whatever time she chooses. This activity never fails to serve up some lively discussion and help us reconnect as a family.

2. On the road. Just consider how much time you spend alone with your child or children in the car in a given week. What better time for asking great questions? After all, you have a captive audience.

3. Bedtime. There are few times during the day when kids are more receptive than when they lie down to sleep.

4. Correspondence. Most everyone enjoys being written to or about, especially kids. One way to give your children a chance to think about their answers is to ask periodic questions in letter form. Place a note in their lunch boxes, tape it to the bathroom mirror, or send it to them in the mail. Few efforts will express your love and interest as well.

5. "Coke dates." Take your son/daughter on a "date." It doesn't have to be expensive to make a big impact.

For example, ask your child in advance; set the time

when you will pick him/her up at school or at home and go out for a milk shake, etc., at a fast-food place. Then use the setting to check in with your child, to see how he/she is doing, to talk about things he/she is interested in, and to ask some great questions. I have often received enthusiastic hugs in return.

6. Family devotions. Taking time to come together in a family meeting at least once a week to read Scripture and pray for each other is a great way to keep a family close and strong. From children's earliest years, parents can adopt creative methods of teaching them the eternal life principles from the Bible. Impromptu dramas, question-and-answer sessions, music, and hands-on projects can illustrate truth and enhance the sense of adventure.

7. In the midst of the storm (literally). Thunderstorms filled most of my South Carolina summers growing up. When the thunder started, my mom practiced something that powerfully affected my view of God. She would turn off all the appliances (TV, radio, washing machine, etc.), turn off all the lights, and get us kids to sit with her on the couch. We'd listen carefully to the claps of thunder, watch the bolts of lightning, and hear the rain beating on our roof.

In those awe-inspiring moments, Mom would wisely ask soul-opening questions: *Isn't God powerful? Can you imagine how strong and mighty He is? Who do you think places the lightning in the sky and sounds the thunder?*

It was in these moments that I came to be deeply impressed with the power and majesty of my mother's God.

8. After church. During the ride home and then during Sunday dinner, go ahead and dig a bit deeper into what your son/daughter absorbed at Sunday school or church. Were there any unanswered questions? Was your child perplexed by anything that was said? This is the time to clear up misunderstandings.

CONCLUSION

When the parenting journey comes to an end, what we have left to hold are the memories we have made with our children. In a moving scene in the film *Dad,* a father (Jack Lemmon) lies on a hospital bed facing a terminal illness. His 30-something son (Ted Danson) asks, "Dad, what are you thinking?"

"I am thinking of all the times I wish I had held you more and told you that I loved you!"

The father's regrets echo those of legions of parents who have tragically missed the moments. Every waking hour is full of opportunities to cultivate closeness with our children and to draw from them their insights, observations, joys, and doubts. Make the most of them. Marshall the questions. Engage their tender souls.

Notes

1. William Beausay II, *Boys: Shaping Ordinary Boys into Extraordinary Men* (Nashville: Thomas Nelson, 1994), p. 97.

2. "We Have This Moment Today." Words by Gloria Gaither; music by William J. Gaither. Copyright © 1975 by William J. Gaither, Inc. All rights controlled by Gaither Copyright Management. Used by permission.

3. Beausay, *Boys,* pp. 102–103.

Chapter Four

LEARNING TO LISTEN

He who answers before listening—
that is his folly and his shame.

Proverbs 18:13

I never learn a thing while I'm talking.
I realize every morning that nothing
I say today will teach me anything,
so if I'm going to learn a lot today,
I'll have to do it by listening.

Larry King, Talk Show Host[1]

Listeners are hard to come by these days. Millions of people spend billions of dollars every year getting professionals to sit and simply listen to their hurts, needs, hopes, and struggles.

Unfortunately, the hurried lifestyles that most parents elect to lead leave little time for the things a child needs most: to be seen, to be gently led, and to be heard.

Don't ask your children questions until you are prepared to absorb what they have to say. To ask and then not listen is to set your child up for disappointment. Children are tough to fool. They tune in to our expressions, emotions, countenance, and general tone. As a result of their tender spirits, our children can tell when we are giving them less than our best attention. Here are some of the giveaways:

Your child knows you're not listening when
- your eyes wander.
- you leave the TV or radio on while

he/she is trying to talk.

- you interrupt in midthought or mid-sentence.
- you keep glancing at a newspaper or magazine.
- you don't ask any follow-up questions.
- you slouch or fold your arms.
- you glance at your watch or a clock.
- you allow noise distractions to compete with efforts to talk to you.
- you finish the child's sentence.

Choosing not to listen actively to our children when they are eager to talk does much more than deprive them of a conversation. It weakens them as individuals. Open and loving dialogue can fill a child's soul with confidence and security.

When a parent fails to listen actively, a child feels

- insignificant.
- frustrated.
- disappointed.
- that the parent doesn't care.
- that maybe someone else will listen better.
- that talking to the parent is a waste of time.
- insecure and uncertain.
- discouraged.
- unimportant.
- unloved and unlovely.
- detached.
- unmotivated to listen to the parent in return.

Great listeners assume nothing. Rather, they ask. They periodically give signals, verbally or nonverbally, that they're following along ("Uh-huh," "I see," "Yes," a nod, etc.). They fully face the person who's talking. "If the speaker is little," say Gary Smalley and John Trent, "it may mean getting down on your knees. Just imagine yourself five-foot-five, living in a world populated by nine-foot giants. It gets tiresome craning your neck all the time!"[2]

Great listeners listen with their hearts, not just their ears. They connect with the feelings being conveyed by the child. They refrain from interjecting their own similar experiences or struggles. They are determined to keep the focus on the child, not themselves.

AM I REALLY LISTENING TO MY CHILD?

How effective are you at listening to your child? The following questions will assist you in getting a sense of how in touch you are with your child's needs, interests, fears, and dreams.

Remember, the greatest question is a waste of energy if not accompanied by a listening ear.

What is weighing on your son's/daughter's mind the most this week?

What in life is your son/daughter currently most excited about?

What is your son/daughter most afraid of at this time?

What is currently your son's/daughter's favorite music group? . . . book? . . . movie? . . . game to play? . . . cartoon? . . . Bible character?

Which talents/hobbies is your son/daughter most interested in?

What friends is your son/daughter currently closest to? What are they like?

What school subjects does your child most enjoy? . . . struggle with?

Which experiences in your child's life thus far have encouraged him/her the most? . . . frustrated him/her the most? . . . hurt him/her the most?

What is the most painful thing anyone has ever said to your child? . . . the most encouraging thing?

The old adage "Children are to be seen and not heard" is flat-out wrong. If Christians applied such thinking to their role as children of God, prayer would be a futile exercise. God's children pray because they are assured of the promise that God will listen to them (Ps. 17:6). If a heavenly Father promises His active attention to the concerns and requests of *His* children, shouldn't earthly fathers and mothers be quick to listen to theirs?

Notes

1. Larry King, *How to Talk to Anyone, Anytime, Anywhere* (New York: Crown, 1994), p. 40.

2. As quoted in Stu Weber, *Along the Road to Manhood* (Sisters, Ore.: Multnomah, 1995), p. 174.

Part Two

THE QUESTIONS

Ask and it will be given to you;
seek and you will find;
knock and the door will be opened to you.
For everyone who asks receives;
he who seeks finds; and to him who knocks,
the door will be opened.

Jesus
(Matt. 7:7–8)

Chapter Five

GREAT QUESTIONS
TO ASK
YOUR
PRESCHOOLER

What is your favorite cartoon to watch? . . . ice cream? . . . toy?

What does Dad/Mom do? *(Get ready—this one might surprise you! My three-year-old son responded, "Moms cook, and dads go outside—and eat!")*

What do you think heaven looks like?

How did you get to be so handsome/pretty? *(Our second daughter has always answered, "Jesus gave it to me!")*

What does God look like?

When you're afraid, what do you do?

Why does Dad/Mom go to work?

Why do we go to church?

What are you thinking about right now?

What does a sad face look like? (*Also try* "happy," "angry," "excited," "afraid," "sweet," "mean," "kind." *Have them show you. This is a great one to do while waiting at a restaurant.*)

Who is the biggest person you know?

Are we supposed to love things, or just like them? What's the difference?

If I asked God to tell me all about you, what would He say?

Are there really angels? Where did they come from? What do they do?

P
R
E
S
C
H
O
O
L
E
R

If you could keep only one of your toys/books, which one would you keep? Why?

How can you make Dad/Mom smile?

How many hugs do you need every day? Why?

What does God do just for fun?

What does sin look like to God?

What is the scariest thing you ever saw?

Where does money come from? How do we get it, and what are we supposed to do with it?

What is your favorite game to play?

Why did God give you hands? What are some good things you can do with them?

What would you like to talk about?

Do you want to be a dad/mom one day? How many kids will you have?

What is the toughest part of being a dad/mom?

What do people do in heaven?

What do you like most about Christmas?

Who is the richest person in the world?

What is your favorite room in our house? Why that one?

P
R
E
S
C
H
O
O
L
E
R

What kinds of things do kids do at school?

What are some things you really don't like?

What is the best thing that ever happened to you?

Who is the strongest person in the world?

What is the most powerful thing God ever did?

What is the prettiest thing you've ever seen?

What would you do if our house caught on fire while you were in it?

How do you feel when it rains and thunders outside?

Have you ever lost something you really liked? What did you do? How did you feel?

What happens to people when they get old?

Where does the sun go at night?

What do you think Dad/Mom liked to do when he/she was a kid?

What do you think first grade will be like?

How many animals do you think Noah had in his ark? What would it be like to spend 40 days and nights with all those animals in one boat? Would you want to do that?

What is the nicest thing you ever did for your sister/brother? Would you do that again?

Why did God give us a Bible? What is it for? How does it help us?

What is the best thing you ever saw on TV? What is the worst thing?

Who are some of your friends? Tell me about one of them. What do they like to play?

Which do you like the best—snow or sunshine? Why?

What makes Dad/Mom unhappy or sad?

Why did God give you feet? What are some good things you can do with them?

How does the sunshine make you feel?

How does the rain make you feel?

What would you do with $5.00?

How many stars are there in the sky?

What do grandpas/grandmas do?

How much do you love Jesus? Show me.

How many hugs do dads/moms need every day?

Why do kids always like to step in puddles?

What is your favorite shirt to wear? Why that one?

Why did God give you eyes? What kinds of things does He want you to see?

What is your favorite story? Would you like me to read it to you right now?

What is the coolest thing you have ever seen?

Who gets to go to heaven?

What kind of animal would you like to be? Why that one?

What is your favorite food?

Why did God give you a voice? What are some good things you can do with it?

What is your favorite song? Would you sing it for me right now?

What is the best surprise you've ever had?

Which color is the happiest color? What makes it so?

Which color is the saddest color? What makes you think that?

Where does bubble gum come from? What is it made of?

Where is the warmest place in our whole house?

If a stranger ever asked you to come with them, what would you do?

Whose house do you like to play at the most? Why that house?

Do you sometimes like being all by yourself? How do you feel when you're alone?

What do you think it was like for Jonah to be in the belly of the huge fish for three whole days? What did it look like? . . . smell like? . . . feel like? Why did he end up there?

What are some things that you like to help Dad/Mom do?

Whom in your family do you look the most like?

What is your favorite snack?

Whom would you like to send a letter to?

How do you know your Dad/Mom loves you?

Which do you like the most—basketball, baseball, or football?

What are some games that boys and girls both enjoy?

What is your favorite Bible story? Would you like me to read it to you right now?

If you had to make breakfast, lunch, and dinner today by yourself for the whole family, what would we be having?

Which one of the Seven Dwarfs reminds you the most of yourself? Why that one?

What is the nicest thing Mom ever did for you?

How many different words do you think you know right now?

What is the newest word you've learned?

What happens when we don't tell people the truth? Do you remember the story about the boy who cried "Wolf!"? Do you want me to tell it to you?

P
R
E
S
C
H
O
O
L
E
R

If your nose grew every time you told a lie, like Pinocchio's, how long would your nose be right now?

How do you feel when someone lies to you?

When do you think you will be old enough to drive a car? What does your mother think?

What is the nicest thing Dad ever did for you?

Can you tell when Dad/Mom is sad? How?

What is the scariest place in our house? Why is it scary to you?

What is your favorite video to watch? Would you like to watch it with me right now?

What is a family? What do families do?

Is there somebody you really miss a lot? Would you like to call him/her on the phone right now?

Who in our family walks the fastest?

Who in our family talks the fastest?

Would you like to go on a date with Dad/Mom today?

How many days are left until your next birthday?

P
R
E
S
C
H
O
O
L
E
R

Chapter Six

GREAT QUESTIONS TO ASK YOUR GRADE-SCHOOLER

What is the best job in the whole world?

What bothers you the most?

If you could go anywhere in the world, where would it be? Why there?

When do you feel the closest to God?

What do you most enjoy doing with your family?

Does school make you feel closer to God or further from Him? Tell me more.

Other than recess and lunchtime, what hour did you most enjoy at school today? Why?

Do you ever feel God talking to your heart? What is it like? What does He tell you in those times?

Do you think the Bible is interesting or boring? What questions do you have about it?

Why do you think God gave you brothers/sisters?

What is sin? What does sin do to people? . . . to families?

What do people do in heaven? Who gets to go to heaven? How do you get there?

What would you do with a million dollars?

Is our family rich or poor?

Why do we have laws/rules?

What happens to people who break the law?

What does the president of the United States do?

What do pastors do? Why?

What is the best time you've ever had with your dad/mom?

What do you like the most about school?

Which day is usually your best day each week? What makes it so special?

How do you decide who your friends will be?

What is the kindest thing anyone ever did for you? . . . said to you?

What is the meanest thing anyone ever did to you? . . . said to you?

If I gave you $10 today, what would you do with it?

What is the greatest thing Jesus ever did?

What is prayer? What does it really do? How should we pray?

If you could become a cartoon character, which one would you want to be? Why?

In the film *Pinocchio*, Jiminy Cricket played Pinocchio's "conscience." What does a conscience do? Where does it come from? Do you have one?

How old do you think you should be to go on your first date? Why then?

How does a Christian date differ from a non-Christian date? What will you do on your first date?

If our family had to move to another state this month, what would you miss the most? Whom would you miss the most?

What are five questions that most kids your age would love to be asked?

Of all the things people have done to you, what has been the toughest thing to forgive? Why?

What is the funniest thing that has ever happened to you?

Who are the three greatest people you have ever learned about? What makes them so great?

What would you do if one of your non-Christian friends said, "I want to become a Christian"? What would you tell him/her?

What is the best gift you've ever given to anyone? What made it so special?

If you could talk to anyone in the world on the phone for 30 minutes, whom would you call? What would you ask them?

What does it mean to be really rich? Exactly how much do you have to have?

What does it mean to be a true friend? Why do you have friends? Do you want more friends?

What are two questions you would really like to ask God?

When you've done something wrong, is it ever hard to say, "I'm sorry"? Why?

GRADE'S CHOOLER

Is there someone in your life you can't stand? What bothers you the most about him/her?

What is your favorite time of the day?

If you could fix your room up any way you wanted, what would it look like?

If you were the dad/mom of the house, what would your top five rules be?

Which do you like more—being alone or being with other people? Why?

Why do wars get started between countries? What stops them?

If you could change one thing about yourself, what would it be?

What is your favorite game to play? Would you like me to play it with you?

If you invited Jesus over to watch TV with you, what programs would He want to watch? Why? What programs would He not want to watch? Why not?

What do you think Grandpa and Grandma were like when they were your age?

What does your name mean? Do you know?

What is the ugliest thing you have ever seen?

Which part of the telephone do you use the most—the transmitter ("talking part") or the receiver ("listening part")? Why?

What would your life be like if there was no television? What would you do more of? . . . less of?

Why is there so much violence on TV and in movies? How does the violence make you feel? How do you think God feels about violence?

What is the saddest thing that ever happened to you?

What is your favorite joke? Would you tell it to me?

When did you feel most embarrassed? Why?

Who is the funniest person you know?

Who is the last person in your school you would want to trade places with? Why?

When is the best time for you to do your homework every day? Why then?

Do you ever remember getting lost? Where were you? How did you feel?

What are some foods that are good for you?

What are some foods that are bad for you?

Why are some things that taste good so bad for your body?

How many hours do you need to sleep every night?

Which outfit of yours are you the most comfortable in?

What is the most amazing thing you ever saw?

GRADE'S SCHOOLER

What is racial prejudice? Have you ever seen it? . . . felt it?

What is a "masterpiece"? Did you know that you are one?

What is wisdom? Where can you find it? Why do you need it?

How can you tell a good choice from a bad one?

What is the most foolish thing you ever did?

If you could be president of the United States for one day, what would you do?

If you could be any one of the characters on the *Star Trek* series, whom would you be? Why that character? Where would you "boldly go"?

Who is someone you feel sorry for? What would you like to do to help him/her?

What do you do when people say things that hurt you?

What happens to people when they die?

What do you think life is like for people who are blind? How would your life be different if you couldn't see?

What subject at school is the most interesting to you?

Why do so many murders take place in our world today when one of the Ten Commandments is "Thou shalt not kill"?

Why do so many kids get involved in gangs? Do you know anyone in a gang? What gets them hooked?

GRADE'SCHOOLER

What is the worst dream you have ever had? Would you tell me about it?

What is the best dream you have ever had? Would you tell me about it?

What do you think you were like when you were a baby? Would you like me to tell you about some of the things you did?

What was the best birthday party you ever went to? What did you like most about it?

When you feel angry, what do you usually do?

What would you do if you knew you had only one month to live?

Which holiday do you like the best? Why that one?

If someone who had never met you before walked into your room, what would your room tell him/her about the kind of person you are?

What is one thing you would be willing to practice at least one hour a day every day until you became great at it?

What is the most expensive thing you own?

What is one thing of yours that you would never be willing to sell at any price?

Is there something you would really like to collect?

What is something Dad/Mom does that you'd really like them to teach you to do?

G
R
A
D
E
'
S
C
H
O
O
L
E
R

Who is your best friend? How did he/she become so special?

Is there someone you would really like to be friends with?

What do you do to start up a friendship?

What are some questions you usually ask someone when you first get to know him/her?

What kinds of things do computers help people do today? What kinds of things do you think we will use computers for when you are Dad's/Mom's age?

What is the most beautiful word in the English language? Why that one?

What do you think high school will be like? How will it be different from your current school?

How do you think Mary felt when God told her she was going to give birth to His Son?

What is the nicest thing your brother/sister ever did for you?

Why do we have judges, lawyers, and courts? What are they for?

Is it important to vote when you become an adult? Does it really make a difference?

When is someone old enough to get married?

Would you like to go to college someday? Which one?

How will getting good grades at school now help you when you're 25 years old?

What does it mean to be generous? Who is the most generous person you know?

What are some different ways to pray?

What is faith? Where does it come from? What can you do with it?

What kinds of things make you cry?

What is the funniest thing you ever saw?

Have you ever said something you wish you could take back? How did you feel?

What is one thing you almost always forget to do?

What is your favorite candy bar? Would you like to go buy one right now?

What is the most difficult instrument in the world to play? *(In an interview, the famed conductor Leonard Bernstein once answered this question tellingly: "Second fiddle.")* Why?

What were you doing at _____A.M./P.M. *(insert a time)* today?

Where do you sit in your classroom? Do you like sitting there? Why or why not?

Which family vacation was your favorite one? What made it so special?

What is one thing Dad/Mom is always trying to teach you?

G
R
A
D
E
'
S
C
H
O
O
L
E
R

What do you think we need to do more as a family?

If you could have only one picture of our family, which one would it be?

Besides exchanging gifts, what is one thing we do as a family at Christmastime that you love and look forward to?

What is one thing you are looking forward to right now?

Chapter Seven

GREAT QUESTIONS TO ASK YOUR TEENAGER

What is "Generation X"? Have you heard anything about it? What do you think it means?

How much do you think it costs, in total, to run this organization called "our family"?

Describe in as much detail as possible the person whom you would like to marry one day. How old is that person today? What is he/she like now . . . personality, friends, ambitions, values?

What are your three favorite songs . . . movies . . . magazines . . . television shows? What do you enjoy the most about them?

When you think about your future, what are you most excited about? . . . afraid of?

What does it mean to be a leader? Do you know any real leaders? Who?

Why do bad things happen to good people sometimes?

Why do good things happen to bad people sometimes?

What do you like the most about being a teenager? What is the toughest part?

What are the three nicest things anyone has ever said about you?

What are the three most hurtful/painful things anyone has ever said to you?

What will you be like when you're 25 years old? Whom do you know that age whom you think you'll be like?

T
E
E
N
A
G
E
R

Who, in your opinion, are the five best role models for teenagers today? What makes them so great?

If God put you completely in charge of creating heaven, what would it look like?

If you didn't have to be concerned about making money and paying bills, what would you most like to do for the rest of your life?

If someone asked you, "How do you know your Dad/Mom loves you?" what would you say?

If you could visit any place you wanted for two weeks, where would you go? . . . with whom?

What three things are you most afraid of?

When can a boy be called a man (or a girl, a woman)?
What does it involve?

What kind of person would you like to be when you're
60 years old? Describe.

What is one thing you've never done that you would
really like to do?

How do you think being a teenager today is different
from when I was a teen? In what way is it similar?
(You may wish to compare yearbooks with your teen.)

If you could live in any other time period in history,
when would you live? Why?

If you knew that next week would be your last week to
live, what are some things you would do?

**T
E
E
N
A
G
E
R**

Why are the Ten Commandments not called the Ten Suggestions?

What is the difference between a Christian family and a non-Christian family?

In your opinion, where should the line be drawn on physical contact with the opposite sex before marriage? Be specific. Why at that point?

What part does God want to play in your life? Where does He fit into the picture?

Do you have doubts or questions about the existence of God? If so, what are they?

What do you think are the most difficult aspects of being a parent?

If you could do anything you wanted to do with your life, and be guaranteed it would succeed, what would you do?

What do you feel the most confident doing? . . . the least confident doing?

What do you most look forward to about growing old? . . . the least?

What does it mean to have integrity or a "good name"? Why is that so important?

How do you feel when someone (even Dad/Mom) breaks a promise he/she has made to you?

When do you feel the closest to your family? . . . furthest from it?

T
E
E
N
A
G
E
R

What is the best time you've ever had with your dad/mom?

Why do so many marriages/families fall apart today? What will you do to make sure yours doesn't?

What are your top three strengths? . . . weaknesses?

Do you feel your life is moving backward, on hold, or moving ahead? In what way?

What does it mean to be popular in your school today? What kinds of things do popular kids do? . . . wear? Who decides who is popular and who is not?

Where do thoughts come from? What is the difference between a good thought and a bad one?

What is the best way to deal with someone who has said or done something to hurt you?

What do you think Jesus was like as a teenager?

How would you define success? What does a successful 25-year-old look like?

Of the following list, which things would be the easiest for you to become addicted to?

Money
Success
Power
Fame
Sex
Alcohol
Drugs
Work
TV

T
E
E
N
A
G
E
R

Do you know how to take a compliment? . . . a criticism?

How will you feel if you get turned down when you ask someone on a date? How will you handle it?

Whom are you the most like—Mom or Dad? In what way? Does that scare you?

What do you like the most about the fact that you're growing older? . . . the least?

What are three needs in your life that I can pray with you about?

What do you think about the job your teachers have? Do your friends respect them? Why or why not?

What are the differences between lust and love?

How will you know when you are really in love?

What does it mean to be a real man? . . . a real woman?

What does television tell you that you "have to have" to be really successful?

What do you think is the most interesting part of the Bible? . . . the dullest part?

What does "cool" mean to you?

What responsibilities will you have 10 years from now that you don't have today? What can you do now to get ready for those?

What bothers you the most about your life?

T
E
E
N
A
G
E
R

How will you know when someone is really in love with you?

If you had to trade places with someone in your school, whom would it be? Why that person?

Do you think Adam and Eve had belly buttons? Think about it.

What makes the Bible more than just an ordinary book?

Which hour of the school day do you most look forward to?

What would you do if you were at home alone and found out a tornado was coming? What if you were baby-sitting?

What is stress? Have you ever felt it?

How do you feel about bungee jumping?

Which one of Dad's outfits is the "coolest"? Which one do you like the least?

What is the most exciting thing that has ever happened to you?

What is the most difficult part of praying?

Are there other Christians on your campus? Who are they? How are they different from non-Christian kids? In what ways are they alike?

What are your five favorite books?

T
E
E
N
A
G
E
R

Which one of Mom's outfits is the "coolest"? Which one do you like the least?

Which of your current classes do you think will help you the most when you're in your thirties? Why?

What is your absolutely favorite restaurant meal? Name the restaurant and the dishes.

Can you give me five great reasons why drinking alcoholic beverages is foolish? Go ahead, list 'em.

Why do we pay some people (say, athletes) so much money, and some (say, waitresses and policemen) so little?

If you had to join the military, which branch would you join—army, navy, air force, marines, or coast guard? Why?

What would you say to a date who pressured you to have sex before marriage? What words would you use?

What kind of work do you think you'll be doing 10 years from now?

What will you have to do to be successful at your work? What will it require from you?

What are five great reasons to wait until you get married to have sex?

If you were being interviewed by your favorite magazine, what five questions would you like to be asked about yourself? What two questions would you not want to be asked?

When you turn 18 and vote in your first election, do you think you will vote Republican, Democrat, or a mixture? Why?

Do you know how to use a checkbook? Would you like me to show you?

Which three people's autographs would you most like to have? Why those three?

What would the ultimate friend be like? Describe him/her to me. Do you have a friend like that?

Is God your friend? In what way?

What do you do to make friends with someone new?

Do you ever get tired of me asking you questions?

Are there any questions you would like to ask Dad/
Mom?

If you could ask God any three questions you wanted,
what would they be?

Are you a "morning person" or a "night person"? How
do you know?

If you had to spend the rest of your life on an island
all by yourself and could have only three things (no
people) with you, what would they be?

What is the most difficult thing you've ever had to do?
What made it so hard?

Would you rather watch an adventure on television or
live one yourself?

T
E
E
N
A
G
E
R

How do you study? What are some of the ways you soak up what you have to learn for a test or class?

What was it that enabled young David to face Goliath, the giant, when all the grown-up soldiers in Israel were afraid to do so? What did he possess that they didn't?

What does it mean to be a "good steward" of your money and possessions? How does God expect you to use your money?

What is the bravest thing you've seen someone do?

What's the difference between courage and foolishness? Explain.

When the going gets tough, what do you usually do?

If you could go back to any day in history and live it yourself, which day would you choose? Why that one?

What are some things you can do to get closer to God?

What motivates you to learn?

What kinds of good come from difficult situations? Can you think of a situation so bad that nothing good could possibly come from it?

What habit would you like to get rid of?

Do you believe in miracles? Have you ever seen one? Would you tell me about it?

If life worked like a videotape player, which button would you use the most—Fast Forward, Reverse, Stop, Play, or Pause? Why that one?

T
E
E
N
A
G
E
R

What do you think Dad's/Mom's biggest problems were when he/she was a teenager?

If moods could be tracked like a weather forecast (e.g., cloudy, partly cloudy, partly sunny, sunny, dreary, rainy, etc.), what would yours be today? . . . this past week?

Is joy something that just comes upon you, or is it a choice/decision?

What are three great things you have going for you as you face the future?

Do you rule your emotions, or do they rule you? In what way?

When we talk, do you feel that I really listen? . . . that I really hear you out? How can you tell when I'm truly listening?

Are there some things you feel you can't ask me? What are some of them?

Have your teachers at school discussed sexuality? What are their opinions and ideas? What do you think about what they are saying?

When you're choosing music, what is most impor-tant—the sound, the lyrics, or the lifestyle the song promotes? How do you decide?

Is abortion ever the right thing to do?

What do you think about the statement "A woman's place is in the home"? Is that true?

What are some of the most tragic things happening in our world today?

What do most kids in your school think about God? . . . about Jesus Christ? What has influenced their opinions of Him the most?

Which comic strip in the newspaper is your favorite? Why do you like that one so much?

How long do you think Adam and Eve lived before they committed the first sin? What makes you think so?

When you meet new people, do you usually assume they will like you, or do you do just the opposite? Why?

What is your favorite Bible verse? Why?

What is the one thing you have always wanted to do?

Conclusion

ASK UP!

As you continue on the adventure of asking great questions, you may wish to turn this into more than an idea book. You may want to make it a memory keepsake as well.

The following pages give you space to record some of your children's more memorable responses. If you write them down, you will find yourself retrieving this volume again and again for years to come just to remember some of the finer moments and to share them as well.

I hope your relationship with your child will be strengthened and enriched by this journey together.

Ask up!

_____

_____

_____

_____

_____

_____

_____

_____

_____

_____

_____

_____

_____

_____

_____

_____

_____

_____

_____

_____

_____

_____

_____

_____

_____

_____

_____

_____

_____

_____

_____

_____

_____

_____

_____

_____

_____

_____

_____

_____

_____

_____

_____

_____

_____

_____

_____

_____

_____

_____

_____

_____

_____

_____

_____

_____

_____

_____

_____

_____

_____

_____

_____

_____

_____

_____

_____

_____

_____

_____

_____

_____

_____

_____

_____

_____

_____

_____

_____

_____

_____

Postscript

A FAVOR TO ASK

I'd like to hear how this book affected your life and parenting experience. Specifically, what questions have you found to be most effective with your preschooler, grade-schooler, or teenager? What questions did you design that proved to be pertinent and soul-opening? What humorous, surprising, or inspiring answers from your child have been the most memorable?

I can't wait to hear from you! Thanks for making this a two-way street.
Send your letters to:

Robert C. Crosby
Christian Center Church
McGinnis Drive
Burlington, MA 01803

Get to Know Your One-and-Only

While the two of you were dating, you probably talked all the time, leaving few subjects untouched. And it can still be that way! ***Now We're Talking! Questions to Build Intimacy with Your Spouse,*** by Robert and Pamela Crosby, will help you keep the conversation flowing and intimacy growing throughout your marriage. It contains hundreds of great questions to encourage both of you to open up and reveal your innermost hopes, dreams, interests, and fears . . . and anything else you can think of! Whether you're celebrating your first year together or your golden anniversary, it's perfect for finding new ways to love and appreciate each other.